*Forever...*

*This book is dedicated
to all my friends,
supporters and readers,
and the love of my life.*

# *THANK YOU!*

# VEGAN SNACK
## 30+ Plant Based Diet Recipes
## (vol. 6)

## *Tasty, Healthy, Amazing*

by Vivian Green

**The Tasty, Healthy, Amazing Collection:**

### Vegan Breakfast
*30+ Plant Based Diet Recipes To Kickstart Your Day*

### Vegan Lunch
*30+ Plant Based Diet Recipes To Keep You Satisfied*

### Vegan Dinner
*30+ Plant Diet Based Recipes To Feel Great at The End of The Day*

### Vegan Dessert
*30+ Plant Based Diet Recipes To Sweeten The Pot*

### Vegan Sauce
*30+ Plant Based Diet Recipes To Spice Your Meals*

### Vegan Snack
*30+ Plant Based Diet Recipes To Stay on Top*

30+ Plant Based Diet Recipes

# Table of Contents

# INTRODUCTION... VEGAN SNACKS

Everybody snacks, even vegans. While eating a whole piece of fruit or a handful of nuts is a great way to hold you over between meals, it can get a bit boring. Whether you want something sweet or savory, the below recipes answer the call of hunger with unique ingredients and fun preparations methods. Most of these can be made in large batches so that you can share your vegan bites with friends.

# SAVORY RECIPES

# Bok Choy Chips

Bok Choy is a variety of Chinese cabbage that is usually steamed, boiled or sauteed and served as part of an entree. Here, it breaks all the rules. Roasting the cabbage gives it a nice crunch that's reminiscent of potato chips but with a much better nutritional profile.

Yields: 2-3 servings

**Ingredients:**

1 – 2 bunches baby bok choy, rinsed well and air dried

2 teaspoons (10 ml) extra virgin olive oil

Fine sea salt, to taste

**Directions:**

Heat your over to 375 degrees F (190 degrees C).

Cut each cabbage leaf in half and place halves into a large bowl.

Add oil and salt. Toss to coat.

Arrange leaves, cut side down, on a sheet pan and bake for 15 minutes or until leaves become crispy.

# Spicy Roasted Chickpeas

Chickpeas (or garbanzo beans) are a vegan staple as they are great sources of vegetable protein. These little legumes are incredibly versatile and can be made into dips (hummus), used in salads or mashed up to create spreads. Roasted, chickpeas are a delightfully crunchy snack that you can carry with you whenever you need a boost of protein.

Yields: 3 servings

**Ingredients:**

1 16 ounce (450 g) can of chickpeas, drained and rinsed

2 teaspoons (10 g) paprika

1 teaspoon (5 g) chili powder

1 teaspoon (5 g) garlic powder

1 teaspoon (5 g) onion powder

1 teaspoon (5 g) salt

1 teaspoon (5 ml) olive oil

**Directions:**

Preheat oven to 350 degrees F (180 degrees C).

Combine all ingredients in a large bowl and toss to coat.

Spread chickpeas in a single layer on a sheet pan.

Bake for 20-30 minutes, stirring several times to ensure even cooking, until chickpeas lose their moisture and shrink a bit.

Remove from oven and allow to cool fully before eating and storing.

# Pizza Bites

This recipe re-purposes tortillas into a satisfying, one bite snack. Perfect for when you're craving pizza but can't commit to an entire pie, these pizza bites are big on flavor but low on calories. You can make up a big batch for a dinner party or just snack on them, one by one, until your craving is satisfied.

**Ingredients:**

1 tablespoon (15 ml) extra virgin olive oil

1 cup (150 g) chopped sweet onion

2 large garlic cloves, minced

1 1/2 cups (225 g) chopped cremini mushrooms

1 cup (150 g) chopped red pepper

one (14-oz/400 g) can crushed tomatoes

3 tablespoons (36 g) tomato paste

1/4 cup (22 g) chopped fresh basil

1 teaspoon (5 g) dried oregano

1/2 teaspoon (3 g) dried thyme

salt & pepper, to taste

large  (9 inch/23 cm) soft tortilla wraps

1/4-1/2 cup (22-45 g) Daiya cheese

## Directions:

Preheat the oven to 375 degrees F (190 degrees C).

Using a round cookie cutter, cut 2.5 inch (6 cm) circles out of the tortillas. Discard (or eat) scraps.

Push each circle into one cup of a mini cupcake tin and bake for 10-12 minutes or until tortillas crisp up.

Meanwhile, make your sauce by first heating the oil in a large skillet over medium heat. Add garlic and onions. Cook for 1-2 minutes until fragrant. Stir in mushrooms and red peppers and continue cooking about 10 minutes, stirring often. Add crushed tomatoes, basil, oregano and thyme. Reduce heat to a simmer and cook until thickened (about 10 minutes).

While the sauce simmers, remove the cupcake tin from the oven and turn it up to broil.

Once the sauce has thickened, fill each tortilla shell with a spoonful of sauce and sprinkle generously with cheese.

Return to oven and broil until the cheese has melted (about 1-2 minutes).

Serve warm.

# Cauliflower Buffalo Wings

Cauliflower is an interesting vegetable that's related to broccoli but has its own special flair. Its hearty texture holds up to a variety of preparations and grabs on to sauces well. While it would be crazy to say that these taste anything like chicken, they do work as a suitable replacement as long as you slather them in enough spicy buffalo sauce.

Yields: 3-4 servings

**Ingredients:**

1 head cauliflower, cut into bite-sized pieces

**Batter**

Dash of your favorite hot sauce

1/2 cup (60 g) brown rice flour

1/2 cup (125 ml) water

Pinch salt

**Sauce:**

1/4 cup (60 ml) hot sauce

1/4 cup (60 ml) canola oil

Pinch salt

**Directions:**

Preheat oven to 450 degrees F (230 degrees C) and lightly coat a cookie sheet with cooking spray.

In a medium bowl, stir together the batter ingredients until smooth.

Dip each piece of cauliflower into batter to coat, shake off excess batter and arrange on cookie sheet.

Bake for 15 minutes or until the batter firms up.

Meanwhile, stir the sauce ingredients together in a small bowl until well-combined.

Remove cauliflower from the oven and brush with sauce.

Return to the oven for about 5 minutes.

Remove from the oven and allow to cool slightly before eating.

# NACHOS

Sometimes the crunchy, layered goodness of nachos is the only thing that satisfies mid-day munchies. With new developments in vegan cheeses and sour cream, vegans need not swear off this Mexican food of the gods. Throw together this recipe for a bowl of satisfying snacking.

Yields: 2-3 servings

**Ingredients:**

1 16 ounce (450 g) can black beans, rinsed and drained

3 tablespoons (36 g) tofutti sour cream

1 avocado

1 plum tomato, diced

1 lime, zested and juiced

1/4 cup (40 g) marinated jalapeno slices

3 ounces (100 g) tortilla chips

1/4 cup (22 g) daiya cheddar, shredded

1/4 cup (40 g) beef-style soy crumbles

1 tablespoon (15 g) taco seasoning

salt and pepper to taste

cilantro sprigs to garnish

**Directions:**

In a medium bowl, mash avocado with lime juice and zest until slightly chunky. Stir in tomatoes and salt and pepper to taste.

In a small bowl, stir together soy crumbles and taco seasoning. Microwave on high for 45 seconds, stirring once.

Place tortilla chips in a large bowl. Top with guacamole, black beans, jalapeno slices, hot soy crumbles, daiya cheese and dollop with sour cream.

Garnish with cilantro.

# BAKED FRIES

Instead of hitting the take out window when you feel like snacking on something starchy, pop on your oven and prepare a homemade snack that's just as good and better for you. Baking fries eliminates the excess oil used when they're deep fried and seasoning them with a little spice adds a welcome kick. This recipe works with any good baking potato like Yukon or Idaho. Try using a sweet potato for even more variation.

Yields: 4-6 servings

**Ingredients:**

4 Russett potatoes, cut into thick evenly-sized wedges

2 tablespoons (30 ml) olive oil

1 1/2 teaspoons (7 g) chili powder

1 teaspoon (5 g) ground cumin

1/2 teaspoon (3 g) ground coriander

Salt and freshly ground black pepper

**Directions:**

Preheat oven to 450 degrees F (230 degrees C) and lightly coat a rimmed baking sheet with cooking spray.

Toss all ingredients together in a large bowl to combine.

Spread potatoes in a single layer on baking sheet and bake for 20 minutes or until crispy and browned.

Remove and allow to cool slightly before eating.

# BEAN CAVIAR

Okay so this neither looks nor tastes anything like fish eggs (which is probably a good thing). The only caviar-esque element this snack captures is a little bit of the round, pop-in-your-mouth, texture of the real thing.

Yield: 4 servings

**Ingredients:**

1/4 cup (60 ml) seasoned rice vinegar

1 tablespoon (15 ml) olive oil

1/4 teaspoon (2 g) salt

1 to 2 jalapenos, seeded and minced

1 clove garlic, minced

1 (15-ounce/420 g) can black beans or black-eyed peas, rinsed and drained

1 large tomato, seeded and diced

1 yellow bell pepper, seeded and diced

1/3 cup (50 g) chopped fresh cilantro or parsley

1/4 cup (40 g) sliced green onions (green and white parts)

**Directions:**

Stir together vinegar, oil, salt, jalapeno and garlic in a large bowl until well-combined.

Incorporate the remaining ingredients and toss to coat.

Serve on top of toasted bread with a dollop of soy yogurt to mimic crème fraiche.

# GRILLED CHICKPEA SLIDERS

Snack burgers are all the rage in the meat-eating world and these vegan versions bring cruelty-free sliders to the snack table. If you can't find mini-buns, subbing a toasted English muffin will do the trick (just shape your patties to fit).

Yields: 8 servings

**Ingredients:**

2 (15-ounce/420 g) (840 g) cans chickpeas, rinsed, drained

1/4 cup (40 g) finely chopped roasted red peppers

3 tablespoons (36 g) vegan mayonnaise

1 tablespoon (12 g) Dijon mustard

2 green onions, minced (white and green parts)

1/3 cup (50 g) finely chopped fresh parsley

3 tablespoons (30 g) whole wheat bread crumbs

1 teaspoon (5 g) chipotle powder

Salt and freshly ground black pepper

8 mini burger buns

Condiments of your choice

Lettuce leaves

Sliced tomatoes

Sliced red onion

**Directions:**

Mash together chickpeas, red peppers, mayonnaise and mustard in a large bowl with a potato masher or fork until a chunky paste forms.

Incorporate bread crumbs, green onions, parsley and chipotle powder. Season with salt and pepper to taste.

With your hands, roll dough into 8 balls and place onto a baking sheet lined with parchment paper. Gently flatten each ball to form a patty and place in the fridge to cool for 10-15 minutes.

Meanwhile, clean, heat and oil the grill.

Grill patties for 3-5 minutes on each side and toast buns on the grill.

Arrange the sliders by spreading a bit of mustard on bottom half of bun. Top each bun with one patty, an lettuce leaf and a slice of both onion and tomato. Spread vegan mayonnaise (or ketchup if you prefer) on the top buns and cover each slider to finish.

# Roasted Red Pepper Dip

If you have a gas stove, roasting your own red pepper is the most rewarding process. All you do is take the whole pepper (remove the sticker if there is one), throw it onto the open flame of the burner and rotate it to get it evenly-charred. It will pop, hiss and generally scare you to death. It will turn black, ugly and look inedible. But in the end, when you remove that pepper from the stove top and dust off the ashes, you will be left with a luscious, perfectly charred pepper that looks like you have a culinary school degree under your belt. Blend your perfect pepper into this dip for a delicious treat you can share with friends.

Yields: 10-12 servings

**Ingredients:**

1 (12 ounce/340 g) package soft tofu

2 cups (300 g) roasted red peppers

1/2 small clove garlic

1/4 cup (40 g) fresh cilantro

1 cup (190 g) vegan mayonnaise

Pinch of chipotle powder

Salt and freshly ground black pepper to taste

**Directions:**

Dump everything in the bowl of your food processor and blend until smooth. Adjust salt and pepper to your liking.

Serve with chips, veggies or a big spoon.

# Jalapeno Poppers

A hot and bubbly cheesy core, surrounded by a spicy, crunchy jalapeno and coated in crispy bread crumbs, it's hard to believe that something so sinful is cruelty-free. Tofutti serves as a perfect cream cheese swap as the texture is indistinguishable.

Yield: 12 servings

**Ingredients:**

12 jalapeno peppers, sliced in half lengthwise, tops and seeds removed

8 ounces (230 g) Tofutti Better Than Cream Cheese vegan cream cheese

1 cup (250 ml) soy milk

1 cup (120 g) flour

1 cup (150 g) bread crumbs

1/4 cup (60 ml) frying oil (like canola or peanut)

**Directions:**

Spoon tofutti into each jalapeno half.

Fill one small bowl with soy milk, another bowl with flour and spread bread crumbs onto a paper plate in a single layer.

Line a baking sheet with parchment paper.

Dip each jalapeno half into soy milk then dredge with flour and arrange on baking sheet to dry.

Immerse dried jalapenos into the soy milk one more time and roll in breadcrumbs.

Return to parchment paper to dry one more time.

Line another baking sheet (or large platter) with paper towels.

Heat oil in a large skillet on medium heat.

Fry jalapenos until golden on both sides (about 3 minutes on each side).

Transfer jalapenos to paper towels to drain for a few minutes before serving.

# CHICKEN FINGERS

Finding the perfect replacement for chicken fingers seems to be a never-ending journey for vegans. This recipe is a good solution for which you can use any mock chicken of your choice. The batter is crispy and seasoned with nutritional yeast to bring out that chicken-y flavor. A hint of mustard gives the fingers a little tang and doubles as a glue that helps the batter stick.

Yield: 4 servings

**Ingredients:**

1 teaspoon (5 g) salt

1/2 teaspoon (3 g) onion powder

1 teaspoon (5 g) pepper

1 teaspoon (5 g) garlic powder

2 cups (240 g) unbleached all-purpose flour

1/4 cup (40 g) nutritional yeast

3 tablespoons (36 g) yellow mustard

1/2 cup (120 ml) water

2 tablespoons (13 g) baking powder

1 pound (450 g) mock chicken

1/2 cup (120 ml) vegetable oil

**Directions:**

In a small bowl, stir mustard and 1/2 of the water together until fully-combined.

In a deep, wide, medium bowl, mix together salt, onion powder, pepper, garlic powder, flour and nutritional yeast. Remove 1/3 cup (40 g) of dry mixture and stir it into the mustard mixture until well-combined.

Incorporate baking powder into dry ingredients.

Working with one piece at a time, dip the mock chicken first into the mustard mixture, shaking off any excess as you remove it. Then, drop it into the dry mixture and dredge until fully coated.

Heat oil in a large skillet over medium heat and fry chicken until golden and crispy (about 3-5 minutes per side).

While the chicken is frying, line a baking sheet with paper towels.

Transfer chicken from skillet to paper towel-lined baking sheet to drain before serving.

# Stuffed Mushrooms

For this recipe, you can use any kind of mushrooms you'd like. For a bigger snack, use portabellas; for entertaining, try either baby bellas or white stuffing mushrooms. Either way, the filling is nutty, cheese-like and delicious.

Yield: 12 servings

**Ingredients:**

1-2 slices bread, toasted and ground in the food processor

2 cloves garlic

12 "stuffing" mushrooms, stems removed and reserved

1/2 cup (75 g)  raw cashews pieces

salt, pepper, onion powder, to taste

2 handfuls spinach

1 handful fresh basil

1/2 cup (75 g) nutritional yeast

**Directions:**

Heat your oven to 350 degrees F (180 degrees C) and lightly coat a glass baking pan with cooking spray.

Combine 1/2 of bread crumbs, garlic, cashews, salt, pepper, onion powder, spinach, basil and nutritional yeast in a food processor and pulse until everything is well-combined. Transfer to a large bowl and drizzle with a little olive oil. Incorporate with your hands.

Stuff each mushroom with filling and arrange on baking sheet.

Sprinkle with remaining bread crumbs over the top and bake for 15-20 minutes until bread crumbs turn golden.

# Hot Tomato Stacks

Most people use tomatoes in cold applications like salads or sandwich fillings. Here the veggie (or fruit, if you're in that school of thought) takes a spin in the oven to create a juicy snack that's layered with the traditional Italian flavors of a caprese salad.

Yield: 2 servings

**Ingredients:**

2 large, ripe garden fresh tomatoes

12 large basil leaves

1/2 cup (75 g) kalamata olives sliced, or olives of choice

about 1/2 cup (about45 g) daiya cheese, mozarella flavor

olive oil

balsamic vinegar

salt and pepper to taste

**Directions:**

Preheat the broiler and line a baking dish with parchment paper.

Slice each tomato in three, thick slices. Trim the rounded tops to make flat slices.

Begin making the stack by placing one slice of tomato on the parchment paper. Top with a sprinkle of cheese, a few basil leaves and olive slices. Add another tomato layer and repeat topping additions. Add final tomato slice, repeat topping additions. Finish by drizzling the stack with a bit of olive oil and sprinkling with salt and pepper.

Repeat process with the rest of the tomato slices and fillings.

Broil in the oven for about 10 minutes or until the cheese is hot and bubbly.

Remove from oven, drizzle with balsamic vinegar and garnish with a few more fresh basil leaves.

# CILANTRO CRACKERS

Great for serving alongside guacamole, salsa or your favorite vegan spread, these crackers are a bit spicy and deliver a refreshing hit of cilantro. While tortilla chips are usually the dipper of choice when it comes to Mexican-themed snacking, these crackers offer an interesting variation that maintains the ethnic flavor profile with a twist.

Yield: 60 crackers

**Ingredients:**

2 cups (240 g) chickpea flour

1/2 cup (60 g) sorghum flour

1/2 cup (60 g) potato starch

1/2 cup (50 g) nutritional yeast

1 teaspoon (5 g) xanthan gum

1 1/4 teaspoon (7 g) salt, divided

1 teaspoon (5 g) red chili pepper powder

1 teaspoon (5 g) cumin

1/2 teaspoon (3 g) coriander

1 teaspoon (5 g) curry powder

1/4 teaspoon (2 g) fenugreek powder

1/3 cup (80 ml) olive oil

1 cup (250 ml) very cold water

additional 1/2 cup (60 g) sorghum flour, plus extra for rolling

1/2 cup (75 g) fresh chopped cilantro

**Directions:**

Heat oven to 350 degrees F (180 degrees C).

In a large bowl, stir together chickpea flour, 1/2 cup (60 g) sorghum flour, potato starch, nutritional yeast, xantham gum, red pepper powder, cumin, coriander, curry powder, fenugreek powder and salt until completely combined.

Stir in olive oil into the dry ingredients until a crumbly mixture forms.

Add water and use your hands to knead the mixture until a sticky dough comes together.

Add remaining 1/2 cup (60 g) sorghum flour and continue to knead until it is incorporated.

Fold in cilantro with your hands until evenly distributed throughout the dough.

Transfer dough to a lightly floured work surface and roll out into a layer about 1/8 inches (3 mm) thick.

Use a cookie cutter to cut crackers and pull away scraps. Lift crackers with a flat spatula and transfer to an ungreased cookie sheet.

Re-roll the scraps and cut more crackers out until you have made about 60.

Bake for 35 minutes or until crackers are golden and crispy.

# EGGPLANT CROSTINI

The grill is a magical cooking tool that imparts its own smokey flavors on just about anything you throw onto it. Grilling eggplant maintains its hearty texture while concentrating its unique flavor. The greek-style soy yogurt acts as a creamy base for the eggplant spread and making it is as simple as placing soy yogurt in a coffee filter over a bowl in the fridge overnight.

**Ingredients:**

1 (1-pound/450 g) eggplant, 1 inch (2.5 cm) slices

1/4 cup (60 ml) extra-virgin olive oil, divided

Cooking spray

16 (1/2-inch/13 mm) slices multigrain baguette

1/2 teaspoon (3 g) salt, divided

2 1/2 tablespoons (38 ml) fresh lemon juice, divided

1/2 cup (95 g) soy yogurt, strained overnight

1/2 teaspoon (3 g) freshly ground black pepper, divided

1 garlic clove, minced

1 cup (150g) arugula

1 cup (150 g) red, orange, yellow, and green cherry tomatoes, quartered

2 tablespoons (20 g)fresh mint leaves, torn

**Directions:**

Preheat grill to medium high.

Brush both sides of eggplant slices with olive oil and grill for 6 minutes on each side.

Brush each bread slice with olive oil and grill for 2 minutes on each side.

Pulse eggplant, salt, 1 tablespoon (15 ml) lemon juice, yogurt, pepper and garlic in a food processor until well-combined.

Spread eggplant mixture evenly over bread slices.

Toss to combine arugula, tomatoes, mint and remaining lemon juice in a small bowl. Drizzle with a bit of olive oil and toss once more.

Add a handful of arugula mixture to the top of every crostini.

# PLANTAIN CHIPS

Plantains are the banana's heartier, more flavorful, big brother. Common to Cuban cuisine, plantains have a sweet flavor but are usually served alongside savory items (like beans and rice). Here, they're made into snackable chips with a quick fry.

Yields: 4 servings

**Ingredients:**

2 cups (500 ml) water

3 cloves garlic, smashed

2 teaspoons (10 g) kosher salt, plus extra for seasoning

1 1/2 cups (370 ml) vegetable or canola oil

2 green plantains, peeled and sliced into 1 inch (2.5 cm) coins

**Directions:**

In a glass bowl, combine water, garlic and salt. Set aside.

Line a cookie sheet with parchment paper.

Using a large pan, heat oil until it reaches 325 degrees F (160 degrees C).

Carefully add plantains to hot oil and fry for 1-1 1/2 minutes on each side. Remove with a slotted spoon and arrange on cookie sheet.

Using the back of a spatula, press excess oil out of each plantain piece.

Transfer plantains to water mixture and soak for about 1 minute.

Remove from water and transfer plantains to an absorbent towel. Press to remove excess moisture.

Return plantains to hot oil and fry until crispy (2-4 minutes).

Line a cookie sheet with paper towels.

Transfer plantains to prepared cookie sheet, sprinkle with salt and allow to drain for a few minutes before eating.

# CURRIED PECANS

Classic Indian flavors are wrapped around each nut to quench your curry cravings between meals. These are great as pops of flavor in salads or by the handful as snacks. Feel free to vary the spices according to your liking using the same technique.

Yield: 12 servings

**Ingredients:**

1 1/2 teaspoons (7 g) onion powder

1 1/2 teaspoons (7 g) garlic powder

1 1/4 teaspoons (6 g) coarse kosher salt

3/4 teaspoon (4 g) curry powder

1/4 teaspoon (2 g) cayenne pepper

2 tablespoons (1/4 stick) (30 g) Earth Balance

2 tablespoons (30 ml) agave syrup

3 cups (450 g)  pecan halves

**Directions:**

Heat oven to 250 degrees F (120 degrees C) and line a baking sheet with aluminum foil.

In a small bowl, stir together onion powder, garlic powder, salt curry powder and cayenne. Set aside.

Add Earth Balance, agave syrup and a pinch of salt to a medium saucepan set over medium heat. When Earth Balance melts, stir in pecan halves until coated and remove from heat.

Stir in spice mixture to coat.

Spread nuts in a single layer on prepared baking sheet.

Bake nuts for 40 minutes or until toasted and fragrant. Allow to cool completely before eating.

# Root Vegetable Chips

Potatoes are the most common root vegetable when it comes to the world of chips. To switch things up, try making chips out of other root vegetables. You will be surprised by the range of flavors different underground veggies offer. The dense sweetness of beets and turnips makes these chips a perfect sweet and salty snack. If you're feeling extra adventurous, you can also try using carrots, daikon, parsnips or rutabagas.

Yields: 4 servings

**Ingredients:**

1 pound (450 g) beets, sliced thinly on a mandolin

1 pound (450 g) turnips, sliced thinly on a mandolin

3 tablespoons (45 ml) olive oil

1/2 teaspoon (3 g) sea salt

1/2 teaspoon (3 g) dried granulated garlic

**Directions:**

Preheat oven to 400 degrees F (200 degrees C) and lightly coat a baking sheet in cooking spray.

In a large bowl, toss vegetable slices with olive oil to coat.

Spread in a single layer on the prepared baking sheet and sprinkle with salt and garlic.

Bake for 20 minutes, turning slices half way through until the vegetables crisp up.

Remove from oven and allow to cool completely.

# Spring Rolls

A light, crunchy snack you can have between meals or as an appetizer, these rolls are easy to make once you master the art of rolling the delicate wrappers. These are filled with traditional Asian spring roll ingredients but you can add avocado or other thinly sliced vegetables, like picked radish, to vary things up. Eat these with your favorite dipping sauce.

**Ingredients:**

10 rice paper or spring roll wrappers

baby greens

baked tofu, sliced into long strips about 1/4 inch (6 mm) wide, the length of the block of tofu

shredded carrots

mung bean sprouts

fresh basil and/or mint leaves

lime

**Directions:**

Fill a large bowl with warm water and set aside.

Rehydrate wrappers by placing them in the water for about 2 minutes, 2 wrappers at a time. Transfer moist wrappers to a paper towel.

Place one re-hydrated wrapper on a dry work surface.

Place a few baby greens, a strip of tofu, carrots, bean sprouts and a few basil or mint leaves to cover the bottom half of the wrapper.

Squeeze lime juice over the filling.

Fold sides of wrapper in and roll upward from the bottom, pressing down gently until you form a roll.

Continue making rolls with the remaining wrappers and filling in this manner.

Serve with your favorite dipping sauce.

# QUICK LETTUCE WRAP

A bit heartier than a spring roll but still light and fresh, these wraps swap out the carbs for a leafy wrapper with a green crunch. The filling is a mix of juicy apples, sweet peach preserves and protein-rich tempeh. Make sure you use Honecrisp apples as their complex flavors are what give this wrap its unique tang.

Yields: 6 rolls

**Ingredients:**

8 ounces (230 g) soy tempeh, crumbled and lightly browned in olive oil

1 large shallot, finely minced

1 cup (150 g) diced English cucumber

2/3 cup (100 g) finely diced Honeycrisp apple

1/2 teaspoon (3 g) sea salt

1 teaspoon (5 g) curry powder

4 drops aromatic bitters

3 tablespoons (36 g) vegan mayonnaise

Scant tablespoon (15 g) peach preserves

6 large leaves of chard, dinosaur kale or green leaf lettuce, rinsed and dried

1/2 teaspoon (3 ml) olive oil

1/8 teaspoon (1 ml) lemon juice

pinch of salt

**Directions:**

In a small bowl, combine lemon juice, oil and salt. Massage each leaf lightly with lemon mixture until slightly softened and pliable.

In a medium bowl, combine all remaining ingredients until well-combined.

Working with one leaf at a time, lay each leaf on a flat, dry work surface and add 1/4 cup (40 g) of filling.

Fold sides of leaves inward and roll up, pressing gently, until you make a roll. Secure with a toothpick at the top.

Continue making rolls with remaining leaves and filling.

Serve with your favorite dipping sauce.

# Pumpkin Hummus

These days, you'd be hard-pressed to find someone that hasn't tried hummus. This Mediterranean staple has made its way around the world, onto people's sandwiches, chips, pita triangles and happily into their mouths. The traditional version is fantastic but if you're looking for a new spin on a delicious classic, this recipe punches it up in both the flavor and color departments. Grab some broccoli florets, celery sticks and a couple baby carrots and dip in like you mean it.

Yields: 8-10 servings

**Ingredients:**

3 1/2 cups (525 g) cooked chickpeas

1 cup (190 g) canned pumpkin puree

2 tablespoons (30 ml) lemon juice

1 heaping tablespoon (20 ml) tahini

2 cloves garlic

1/2 to 3/4 cups (120-180 ml) water

1 to 2 tablespoons (15-30 ml) chili garlic sauce

1 tablespoon (15 ml) olive oil

sea salt to taste

**Directions:**

Pour 1/2 cup (120 ml) of water in the bowl of a food processor then add remaining ingredients.

Process for 10 minutes or until the mixture is fluffy. Add more water to thin as necessary.

Transfer to an airtight container and chill for about 3 hours before serving.

# FRENCH ONION TWISTS

These little crispy bites are great for a party or whenever you're in the mood for a bit of crunch. By draining the soy yogurt overnight, you are essentially creating Greek-style yogurt, a thick version of the runny regular that is much creamier. The French onion flavor is easily re-created with soup mix which includes the right blend of herbs and spices to give these twists a lot of character.

Yields: 10-12 servings

**Ingredients:**

2 sheets of  puff pastry

16 ounces (450g) unsweetened soy-yogurt

1/2 - 3/4  package organic onion soup powder

3 tablespoons (45 g) poppy seeds

**Directions:**

Place a coffee filter into a fine mesh sieve and place the sieve over a bowl, making sure it doesn't touch the bottom. Add yogurt and strain in the fridge overnight.

Remove strained yogurt from fridge and transfer to a small bowl. Stir in 1/2 package of onion soup powder. Taste for flavor and adjust with more powder as necessary. Return to the fridge to cool while you prepare the pastry dough.

Preheat oven to 400 degrees F (200 degrees C) and line a baking sheet with parchment paper.

Roll out each pastry dough sheet.

Spread yogurt mixture thinly onto one dough sheet and cover with the other, pressing gently to seal.

Cut the dough into even strips.

Spread poppy seeds onto a dry work surface and lightly roll each strip in seeds, pressing gently so they attach.

Twist each strip and arrange, 1 inch (2.5 cm) apart, on the prepared baking dish.

Bake for 20 minutes or until twists are puffed and golden brown.

Cool slightly before serving.

# Zucchini Muffins

These herbed muffins are perfect portable snacks. Zucchini pieces and daiya cheese are strewn throughout this moist, crumbly treat. Have one straight from the oven with a nice slather of Earth Balance.

Yields: 12 muffins

**Ingredients:**

1/4 cup (60 ml) olive oil

1 teaspoon (5 g) cumin

2 cloves garlic, minced

1 teaspoon (5 g) fresh thyme, minced

1 teaspoon (5 g) fresh rosemary, minced

1 green onion, sliced into small bits

2 small zucchini, peeled and shredded (about 1 cup/150 g)

1/2 cup (45 g) cheddar style Daiya vegan cheese, packed

1 cup (120 g) sorghum flour

1/4 cup (30 g) almond flour

1/4 cup (40 g) finely ground yellow corn meal

1/2 cup (60 g) potato starch

1/2 cup (75 g) nutritional yeast

1 teaspoon (5 g) xanthan gum

2 teaspoon (10 g) baking powder

1 teaspoon (5 g) baking soda

1/2 teaspoon (3 g) salt

1 cup (250 ml) unsweetened almond milk

3 tablespoons (45 ml) vinegar

additional Daiya for sprinkling

**Directions:**

Heat your oven to 350 degrees F (180 degrees C) and line a 12 cup muffin tin with muffin liners. Lightly dust them with sorghum flour as well.

In a medium bowl, stir together olive oil, cumin, garlic thyme, rosemary, green onion, zucchini and 1/2 cup (45 g) of cheese.

In a large bowl, combine flours, corn meal, potato starch, nutritional yeast, xantham gum, baking powder, baking soda and salt.

Stir zucchini mixture into flour mixture gradually until large lumps disappear. Thin with almond milk gradually until the entire cup is incorporated.

Add vinegar 1 tablespoon (15 ml) at a time, mixing to combine after every addition.

Fill each muffin cup 3/4 of the way up with batter.

Sprinkle more cheese over the top of each muffin.

Bake for 20-25 minutes or until muffins are dry to the touch but not browned.

Serve warm.

# GUAC IN CUPS

At parties, the guacamole usually lives in a large, uneventful bowl. These single serving cups utilize the avocado shell as a serving vessel, which eliminates the need for you to wash that big party bowl when the celebration comes to an end. Top it off with your favorite hot sauce and set the fiesta in your mouth a'blazin'.

Yield: 8 servings

**Ingredients:**

4 medium to large ripe avocados, halved crosswise, pit removed

2 tomatoes, seeded, chopped

1 tablespoon (15 g) lime zest

Juice of 2 limes

Pinch of salt

Pinch of sugar

A few grinds black pepper

1/3 cup (50 g) finely chopped fresh cilantro

**Directions:**

Run your paring knife along the edges of each avocado. Holding one half in your hand, carefully cut the avocado flesh into cubes, making sure you don't pierce the flesh. Scoop out cubes with a spoon into a large bowl and set the shells aside.

Stir in remaining ingredients until well-combined, leaving some texture by not fully mashing the avocado.

Spoon guacamole back into avocado shells and serve with hot sauce and chips.

SWEET

# Peanut Butter Strawberry Tacos

When you've run out of taco filling but have plenty of tortillas hanging around, make this sweet snack to efficiently dwindle down the stack. Not your average taco, these are filled with a quick homemade strawberry jam that melts the peanut butter inside the slightly charred tortilla. A drizzle of vegan chocolate sauce or a bit of vegan whipped cream wouldn't hurt as a topper here.

Yields: 8 servings

**Ingredients:**

8 ounces (230 g) fresh strawberries, hulled

3 tablespoons (45 ml) agave nectar

8 whole-wheat, taco-sized tortillas

1/2 cup (120 g) crunchy or creamy all-natural peanut butter

**Directions:**

In a medium saucepan set over medium heat, stir together strawberries and agave syrup. Cook for about 10 minutes or until the strawberries begin to break down and the mixture thickens.

Place 1 tortilla directly over the flame of a gas burner. Char for about 1 minute and flip with tongs. Char on the other side for about a minute.

Spoon 1 tablespoon (15 g) of peanut butter into the center of the tortilla and top with 1 tablespoon (15 g) of strawberry jam. Fold over to create taco.

Continue making tacos in this manner until you have used all of the tortillas and filling.

# Dark Chocolate Apricots

Apricots are super high in potassium (one serving is comparable to a banana) and make for a great mid day pick me up. Slapping a little bit of dark chocolate on them boosts this snack's antioxidant content and makes it taste decadent enough to be dessert.

Yield: 6 servings

**Ingredients:**

1 (7-ounce/200 g) package dried apricots

1/2 cup (70 g) dark chocolate chips

1/4 cup (20 g) salted cashew halves

**Directions:**

Line a cookie sheet with parchment paper.

Melt the chocolate in a double broiler (or in a microwave safe bowl in 30 second intervals to prevent scalding).

Dip each apricot into the chocolate and arrange on the parchment paper.

Top each apricot with a cashew while the chocolate is still pliable and allow the chocolate to harden before eating.

# Choco-Cherry Granola

Granola this good should almost be considered candy. Good-for-you oats are baked up with an array of delicious accompaniments like coconut, chocolate and cherries that all melt together to create a luxurious snack. Add a handful to some soy yogurt and use it as a quick hit of sweet energy.

Yields: 6 servings

**Ingredients:**

1/2 cup (120 ml) pure maple syrup

1 vanilla bean, split and scraped

3 cups (300 g) rolled oats (not quick cooking or instant)

1/4 cup (25 g) baking cocoa

1/4 cup (60 ml) vegetable oil

1/2 cup (45 g) shredded, unsweetened coconut

1/2 cup (75 g) slivered almonds

Pinch of salt

1/2 cup (75 g) dried cherries

**Directions:**

Heat your oven to 300 degrees F (150 degrees C).

Spread the oil on a rimmed baking dish and place in the oven to warm for about 10 minutes.

Warm the maple syrup in a small saucepan over medium heat for about 3 minutes and stir in vanilla bean and its seeds. Simmer for 2 minutes until fragrant then remove from heat.

In a medium bowl, stir together oats and cocoa until well-combined.

Transfer to oiled baking sheet and spread into an even layer. Bake for 10 minutes.

Incorporate coconut, salt and almonds. Return to oven and bake for 5 minutes.

Take vanilla bean out of the maple syrup mixture and pour over granola. Stir in cherries until everything is well-coated.

Return to oven and bake for a final 10 minutes, stirring occasionally.

Remove from oven and allow to fully cool before eating.

# Mango Protein Smoothie

A well-balanced snack should contain a good amount of both protein and carbohydrates with a little fat to help your body absorb the nutrients. This smoothie qualifies as a post-gym revival snack, is loaded with vitamin C and tastes fantastic. Blending tofu into the smoothie ups the protein substantially and adds a thicker, more velvety texture. Feel free to throw in some berries for an antioxidant boost.

Yields: 1 serving

**Ingredients:**

4 ounces (113 g) of soft tofu, drained

1/2 cup (120 ml) orange juice

1 1/2  cups (225 g) frozen mango

3 tablespoons (45 ml) agave syrup

1/2 cup (120 ml) dairy-free milk

**Directions:**

Puree everything in a blender for 1-2 minutes. That's it.

# RICE KRISPIES TREATS

Aside from the cereal, marshmallows and butter are the main ingredients in traditional rice krispies treats. This vegan version is made dairy-free (and a ton healthier) by subbing almond butter as the binder. To add another layer of delicious, a bit of chocolate is drizzled on top.

Yields: 12 servings

**Ingredients:**

1/2 cup (120 g) chunky almond butter

1/2 cup (120 ml) brown rice syrup

1 tablespoon (15 ml) pure vanilla extract

1 tablespoon (15 g) Earth Balance

1/2 teaspoon (3 g) kosher salt, or to taste

3 1/2  cups (315 g) Rice Krispies Cereal

**Chocolate drizzle**

1/4-1/2 cup (35-70 g) chocolate chips

1 tablespoon (15 g)  almond butter

pinch salt

Shredded coconut, to garnish

**Directions:**

Line an 8 inch by 8 inch ( 20 cm x 20 cm) pan with parchment paper.

Stir together Earth Balance, brown rice syrup, almond butter and salt in a medium saucepan set over medium-low heat until Earth Balance melts and everything is smooth.

Remove from heat and incorporate vanilla extract.

Using a wooden spatula, incorporate the cereal until coated with butter mixture.

Turn out onto prepared pan and using your hands, pat the mixture to evenly distribute. Put into the freezer for 5 minutes to set.

Melt chocolate chips in the microwave in a medium bowl, heating in 30 second intervals to prevent scalding.

When chocolate is melted, incorporate the salt and almond butter.

Drizzle chocolate glaze over rice mixture and return to the freezer for 15 minutes or until chocolate hardens.

Cut treats into 12 squares with a sharp knife.

# PROTEIN BARS

Protein is essential in everyone's diet but getting a good amount of protein as a vegan is a little tricky at first since you cut out all the traditional sources like meat and eggs. These bars are great as a post-workout snack and are filling enough to serve as breakfast. Throw one in your gym bag and go.

Yield: 10 bars

**Ingredients:**

1 cup (100 g) rolled oats

1 cup (90 g) brown rice crisp cereal

1/4-1/2 cup (25-50 g) protein powder

1/2 teaspoon (3 g) ground cinnamon

pinch of salt

1/2 cup (120 ml) brown rice syrup

1/2 cup (120 g) sunflower seed butter

2 teaspoons (10 ml) vanilla extract

1/3 cup (45 g) dark chocolate chips, melted

**Directions:**

Stir together oats, cereal, protein powder, cinnamon and salt in a large bowl.

Combine rice syrup and sunflower seed butter in a smaller bowl and microwave for 30-40 seconds to soften the mixture. Incorporate vanillas extract.

Stir wet ingredients into the dry ingredients and use your hands to mix everything together until a thick dough forms.

Turn dough out into a baking dish and spread out evenly. Use a roller to smooth out the top.

Place chocolate chips in a small bowl and microwave until melted (about 20 seconds).

Spread chocolate evenly across the top of the dough.

Place in the freezer to set for 10 minutes then cut into 10 bars using a sharp knife.

# BALSAMIC BASIL PEACHES

This snack is a sweet celebration of summer, with a little fancy twist. Peaches are best at the beginning of August, which happens to be a great month to grill outside. The natural sugars in tree-ripened peaches caramelize beautifully when they hit the hot grill and the fresh, herbal taste of basil and tangy balsamic vinegar contrast to maximize the fruit's sweetness.

Yield: 6 servings

**Ingredients:**

6 large, ripe peaches, pitted and halved

1/2 cup (120 ml) balsamic vinegar

2 tablespoons (25 g) sugar

4-6 large leaves fresh basil, cut in chiffonade

**Directions:**

Preheat the grill to high.

In a small saucepan over medium heat, combine balsamic vinegar and sugar. Bring to a slow boil and reduce heat to low. Allow to simmer until the liquid reduces by about half and becomes syrupy (about 10-15 minutes).

Remove from heat and set aside to cool completely. When cool, transfer to a squeeze bottle.

Grill peaches cut side down for about 5 minutes or until grill marks appear.

To serve, arrange peaches cut side up, drizzle with 1 tablespoon of balsamic glaze and sprinkle  with basil.

# OAT BARS

Many energy bars available in stores have a whole slew of ingredients you've never heard of or, in the alternative, the good-for-you bars are super expensive. Well, these bars are incredibly easy to make, have very few ingredients and are a great energy booster whenever you're feeling down. As a bonus, they will save you some big bucks if you just put in a little bit of prep work.

Yield: 9 servings

**Ingredients:**

2 large, very ripe bananas, peeled
1 teaspoon (5 ml) vanilla
2 cups (200 g) rolled oats
1/2 teaspoon (3 g) salt
1/4 cup (40g ) pitted, chopped dried dates
1/4 cup (40 g) chopped walnuts

1/2 teaspoon (3 g) nutmeg

1/2 teaspoon (3 g) cinnamon

**Directions:**

Preheat oven to 350 degrees F (180 degrees C) and lightly spray a 9 inch x 9 inch (23 cm x 23 cm) baking pan with cooking spray.

In a medium bowl, mash the bananas until smooth with a potato masher or fork.

Stir in remaining ingredients until well-combined.

Turn out mixture into the baking pan and press to evenly distribute.

Sprinkle a bit of cinnamon over the top.

Bake for approximately 30 minutes or until the edges begin to pull away from the baking dish.

Cool on a wire rack and cut into 1 inch x 1 inch (2.5 cm x 2.5 cm) squares with a sharp knife

# Peachetta

Traditional brushetta is vegan but when you're sick of the same tomato routine, switch it up by adding some fresh peaches to the tomato topping. The key here is to use ripe, but firm, peaches to get the best texture. These are especially nice with a mid-morning mimosa.

Yield: 4-6 servings

**Ingredients:**

1 (8-ounce/230 g) baguette, cut crosswise on a diagonal into slices

Extra virgin olive oil

1 large clove garlic, halved

2 ripe but firm peaches, halved, pitted, chopped

2 ripe roma tomatoes, halved, seeded, chopped

1/3 cup (50 g) finely chopped onion

2 tablespoons (20 g) finely chopped fresh parsley

2 tablespoons (20 g) finely sliced basil leaves

Salt and freshly ground black pepper to taste

**Directions:**

Brush the baguette slices with olive oil and rub them with a garlic half to impart flavor.

Toast bread in a 400 degree F (200 degrees C) oven until lightly crispy (about 10 minutes).

Remove from oven and allow to cool completely.

Dice garlic and place into a large bowl with the remaining ingredients. Toss to combine then drizzle a bit of olive oil to coat. Season with salt and pepper to taste.

Distribute bruschetta mixture evenly on top of cooled toasts.

# WATERMELON JALAPENO SALSA

A world apart from boring tomato salsa, this refreshing recipe pairs spicy jalapeno with succulent watermelon to create a mouth-watering salsa that's perfect when you're craving a little spice. Mango is used to round out the fruity flavor but can be subbed for tomatillos if you want something a bit more savory.

Yields: 4 servings

**Ingredients:**

2 cups (300 g) (1/2-inch/13 mm) cubed seeded watermelon

1 cup (150 g) (1/2-inch/13 mm) cubed peeled ripe mango

1/4 cup (40 g) finely chopped red onion

2 tablespoons (20 g) chopped fresh cilantro

2 tablespoons (20 g) finely chopped seeded jalapeño pepper (about 1 small)

1 tablespoon (15 ml) fresh lime juice

1/2 teaspoon (3 g) sugar

1/4 teaspoon (2 g) salt

**Directions:**

Combine all ingredients in a medium bowl and mix to combine.

Refrigerate for at least 2 hours before serving to allow the flavors to marinate.

# THANKS!

This is it!

That is the final book of the Tasty, Healthy, Amazing collection. You now have all of my best recipes, but above all these are now YOUR recipes.

THANK YOU so much for your support. I took me time to get these meals out and at some point they may never have been published. It took some effort and the love of my close ones to finally share some vegan love with the world.

Looking back, the 30+ Plant Based Diet Recipes experience has been awesome to write, but even more to cook every day. I wish you get the same great time sharing your preparation with your friends and your family.

If you followed my adventure from the Breakfast book to the final one (this Snack recipes collection), then you now have over 200 recipes!

So it is time for me now to say Goodbye, and again:

Thank you, thank you, THANK YOU.

      Vivian ;)

# The Tasty, Healthy, Amazing Collection:

### Vegan Breakfast
*30+ Plant Based Diet Recipes To Kickstart Your Day*

### Vegan Lunch
*30+ Plant Based Diet Recipes To Keep You Satisfied*

### Vegan Dinner
*30+ Plant Diet Based Recipes To Feel Great at The End of The Day*

### Vegan Dessert
*30+ Plant Based Diet Recipes To Sweeten The Pot*

### Vegan Sauce
*30+ Plant Based Diet Recipes To Spice Your Meals*

### Vegan Snack
*30+ Plant Based Diet Recipes To Stay on Top*

## 30+ Plant Based Diet Recipes

Made in the USA
Monee, IL
18 November 2019